LEARN TO DRAW

Phineas and Ferb

Phineas and Ferb created by Dan Povenmire and Jeff "Swampy" Marsh

Illustrated by Greg Guler and Nancy Ulene

Written by Scott Peterson

7 9 10 8 6

Table of Contents

There are 104 days of summer vacation, and each of those days is as precious as aglets (you know, those little stoppers at the end of your shoelaces) to stepbrothers Phineas Flynn and Ferb Fletcher. Their goal is to make the most of every day, filling their summer with cool inventions, wild adventures, and—for some reason—giant, floating baby heads.

Phineas Flynn has a way with words and an unlimited imagination. If he can dream it, he can do it. And he usually does. Ferb Fletcher is more a man of action, letting his deeds speak for him…but when he does speak, it's worth listening to. Together they have created some of the greatest spectacles their hometown of Danville has ever seen…but their mother has not.

"Ferb, I know what we're gonna do today," Phineas says each morning before they launch into that day's project. Whether it's building

the world's biggest roller coaster, a robot rodeo, or a pickle the size of Pluto, there is no limit to what they can do. They've wrangled cattle through a mall, stopped an alien bounty hunter, and even traveled through time. Twice! You might ask, "Aren't they a little young to do all this?" Yes, yes, they are. (The fact that you are asking questions of a book is a bit odd, but we'll ignore that for now.)

But they aren't alone in their quest for the best day ever. Helping them with their fun are their three best friends, Buford Van Stomm, Baljeet Rai, and Isabella Garcia-Shapiro. Buford is known as a big bully, although he saves most of his wedgies for Baljeet. Baljeet is highly intelligent and obsessed with education and grades. Isabella, on the other hand, is the self-assured leader of the Fireside Girls. She splits her time between earning merit patches with her troop and helping Phineas and Ferb. Well,

mostly helping Phineas. She has a major crush on him.

Unfortunately, there is one major obstacle to the kids' fun-seeking efforts: the Abominable Snowman! (No, not really.) It's Phineas and Ferb's older sister, Candace Flynn. She thinks the crazy things they do are dangerous, abnormal, and just not right. She believes it's her duty to reveal her brothers' shenanigans to their mother and bust them. And she is more than a little obsessed. Other than her crush, Jeremy Johnson, Candace thinks of nothing but busting Phineas and Ferb 24-7. She often mutters to herself, "They're going down, down, down."

Candace has tried everything in her drive to bust the boys: Gathering evidence. Taking pictures. Even yanking her mom from the

shower and carrying her to the backyard to see what the boys are doing. But it never works out for Candace.

Part of the problem is that her mom, Linda Flynn-Fletcher, is a very busy woman. She is raising three kids; supporting her husband, Lawrence Fletcher, at his antique store; running errands; and taking every adult education class offered in Danville. She doesn't have time to drop everything and run home every time Candace calls. By the time Mom does get home, the boys' inventions have somehow disappeared, and Candace is defeated once again.

The one remaining member of the Flynn-Fletcher family is their pet platypus, Perry. This blue-green creature with his webbed feet, duck-like bill, and beaver tail is one of only a

few semi-aquatic, egg-laying mammals on the planet. (For more information, visit your local library!) These creatures are very interesting looking, but they don't do much.

Except that this platypus is also a secret agent. When Perry slaps on his trademark fedora, he becomes a crime-fighter known as Agent P. No one in the family knows about his double life, and when he's off on a mission, they can often be heard asking, "Hey, where's Perry?"

Perry belongs to the OWCA (Organization Without a Cool Acronym). It is filled with animal agents who work to stop evil in the Tri-State Area. Major Monogram is Perry's immediate supervisor. When Perry slips through a secret panel and slides down a tube into his underground lair, it is Major Monogram that's waiting there to give him his assignment: Stop Dr. Doofenshmirtz!

Dr. Heinz Doofenshmirtz is Perry's long-time nemesis. Originally from the small town of Gimmelshtump in the Eastern European nation of Druselstein, Dr. Doofenshmirtz now resides in the penthouse suite of Doofenshmirtz Evil Incorporated in downtown Danville. He lives with a robot named Norm, has a teenage daughter named Vanessa, and is a member of an evil society called L,O,V,E M,U,F,F,I,N. He also loves old cheese, long walks on the beach, and peanut brittle.

Doof's primary focus in life is evil. Each day, Perry breaks in to stop Dr. Doofenshmirtz's latest evil plan and gets trapped in one of Doof's ingenious traps. Doof then takes the time to explain his entire evil plan to take over the Tri-State Area. Not the world—he likes to start with manageable goals. Then he reveals his latest diabolical invention. He calls these inventions "inators" and has built some very unusual ones,

including a ballgown-inator, a de-love-inator, an everything-evil-inator, a hot-dog-revenge-inator, and even a monkey-enslav-inator.

In the end, Perry always prevails, stopping the scheme and destroying Doof's inator.

Perry rockets away as Doof yells, "Curse you, Perry the Platypus!"

Strangely enough, Doof and Perry's actions usually intersect with Phineas and Ferb's plans for the day, often taking away whatever they have created before their mom can see it. The boys don't mind because it helps with clean up and besides, they've already had their fun.

So now that you know a little bit about the world of Phineas and Ferb, pick up a pencil and start drawing them. Draw! Draw like the wind, my friend! "Seize the day," as Phineas would say, because summer is

short, and it's your job to make the most of it. So stick with us 'cause Phineas and Ferb are gonna do it all!

Tools & Materials

Before you begin drawing, you will need to do what Ferb does and gather the right tools. Start with a regular pencil, an eraser, and a pencil sharpener. When you're finished with your drawing, you can bring your characters to life by adding color with crayons, colored pencils, markers, or even watercolor or acrylic paints!

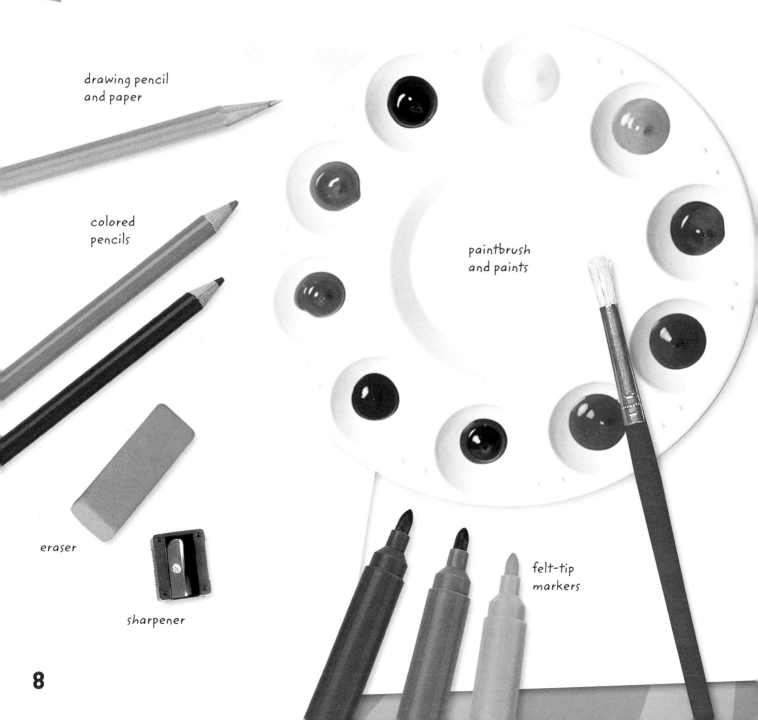

drawing pencil and paper

colored pencils

paintbrush and paints

eraser

sharpener

felt-tip markers

Getting Started

Professional artists draw characters in steps. The key is to start with simple shapes and gradually add the details. The blue lines will help guide you through the process.

1

First you'll draw guidelines to help position the character's features.

2

Next, you'll start to add details. It will take several steps to add them all.

3

When you finish adding the details, erase your guidelines. Then darken your final sketch lines with a pen or a marker.

Size Comparison Chart

Check out how big (or small) the characters are. Use Phineas and Ferb as a guide for comparing the height of the other characters.

Phineas Flynn

Phineas is the most creative, triangle-headed kid that you'll ever meet. Full of ideas and a sense of adventure, there is nothing he won't try to wring the most fun from his summer.

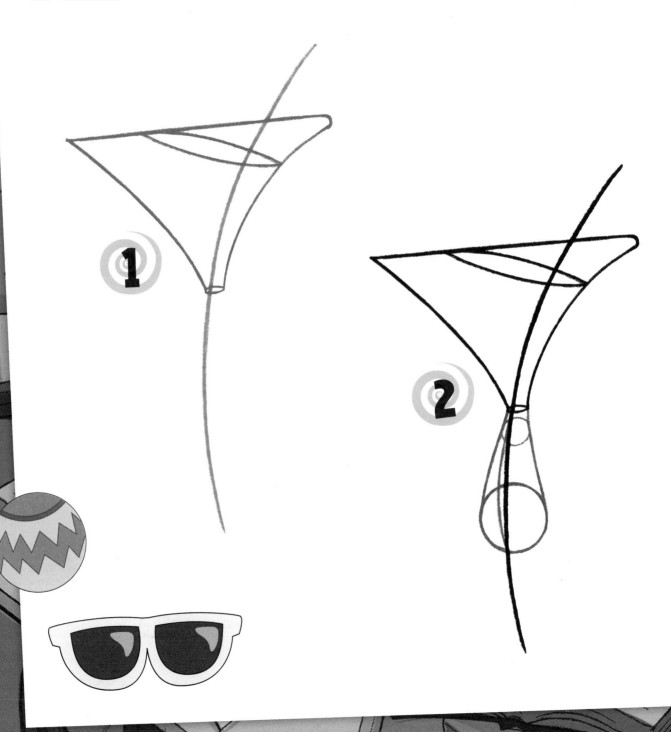

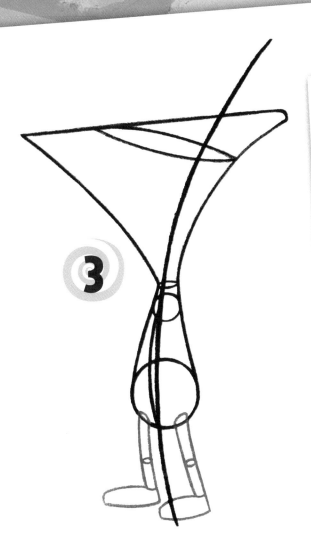

3

KEEP
THE BACK
OF HIS
HEAD
CURVED

PHINEAS
HAS A SLIGHT
CHIN

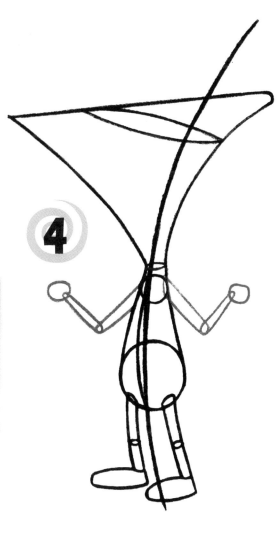

4

KEEP A
SLIGHT CURVE
TO HIS LEG

NO SOCKS...
JUST HIGH TOPS—

WHO KNEW PHINEAS WAS
SUCH A FASHION PLATE?

3
2
1
4
5
6

THE DOTS
ON HIS HEAD
FORM A
TRIANGLE

BUT TECHNICALLY, ANY
THREE DOTS FORM A
TRIANGLE, SO...

5

6

3

NOTE THAT ALL
PHINEAS AND FERB
CHARACTERS HAVE A
"3" TO INDICATE THE
DETAIL OF THE EAR,

UNLESS THEY ARE FACING
RIGHT, IN WHICH CASE THEY
HAVE AN "E" FOR THE EAR

Ferb Fletcher

Ferb is an inventor extraordinaire, never far from his blueprints and tools. He speaks quietly, but carries a big blowtorch. He is calm in a crisis, and nothing distracts him from the task at hand…except maybe for Vanessa—Dr. Doofenshmirtz's too cool daughter.

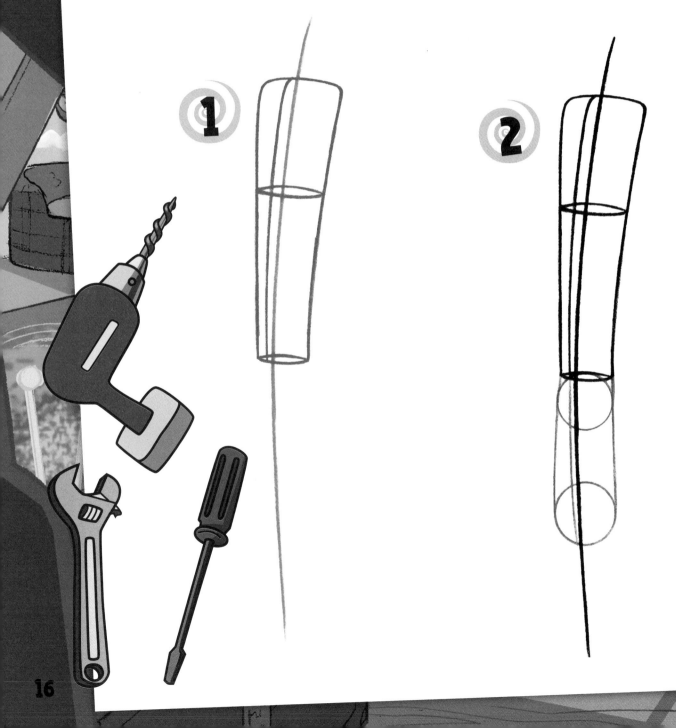

③

④

FERB'S HEAD
AND BODY ARE
SHAPED LIKE A
BASEBALL BAT
STUCK INTO A
TEST TUBE

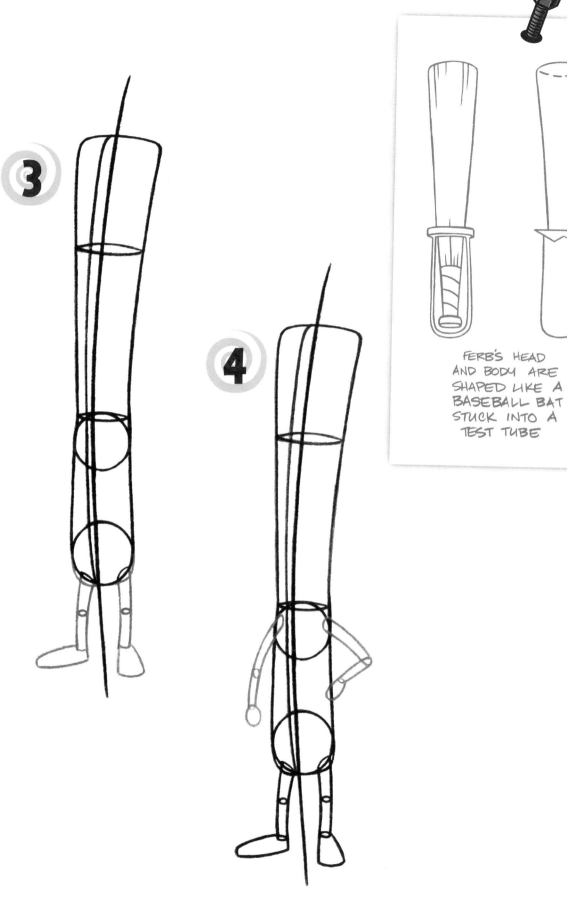

NOT THIS...   ...THIS!

ALL CHARACTERS IN "PHINEAS AND FERB" HAVE SLEEVES THAT COME TO POINTS... THEY ARE <u>NOT</u> ROUND

CLEARLY, MOM IS USING TOO MUCH STARCH

5

6

CENTER OF COLLAR WEDGE, BUTTON, AND BELT BUTTON FOLLOW CENTER LINE ON BODY

SLEEVES TAPER INTO BODY

Candace Flynn

Candace is a high-strung teenager obsessed with busting her brothers. She loves her bros, but she desperately wants to prove to her mom that they are up to something. Sadly, she is her own worst enemy. (Oh, and she has an unusually long neck.)

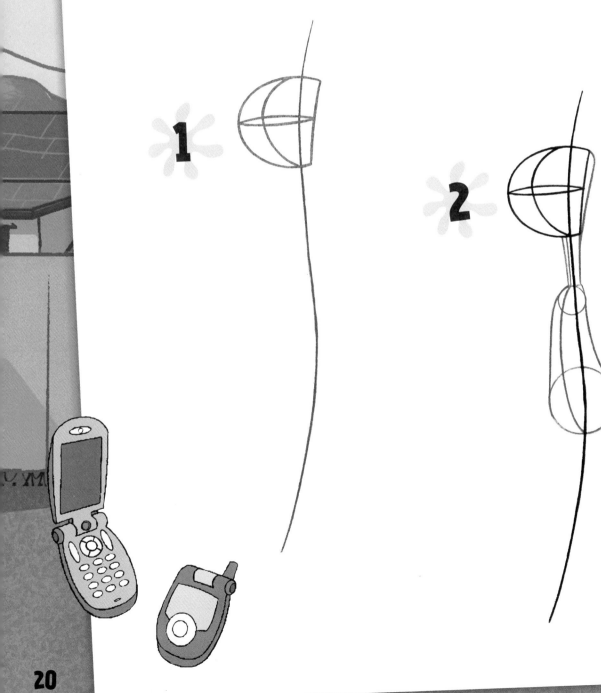

3

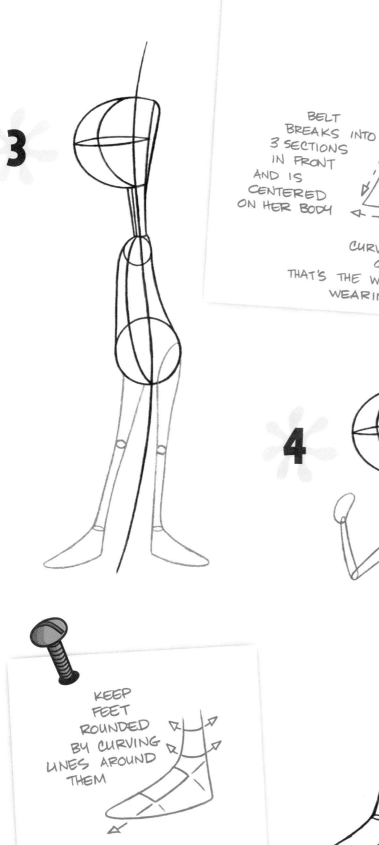

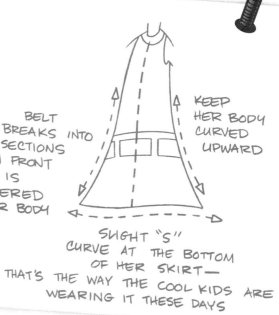

BELT
BREAKS INTO
3 SECTIONS
IN FRONT
AND IS
CENTERED
ON HER BODY

KEEP
HER BODY
CURVED
UPWARD

SLIGHT "S"
CURVE AT THE BOTTOM
OF HER SKIRT—
THAT'S THE WAY THE COOL KIDS ARE
WEARING IT THESE DAYS

4

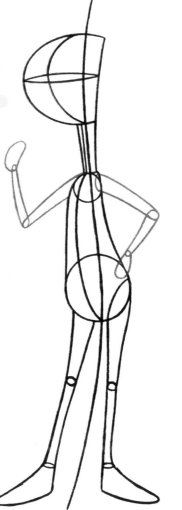

KEEP
FEET
ROUNDED
BY CURVING
LINES AROUND
THEM

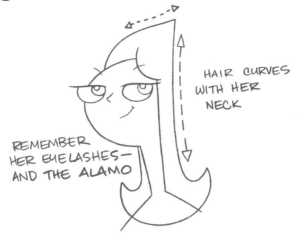

HAIR CURVES
WITH HER
NECK

REMEMBER
HER EYELASHES—
AND THE ALAMO

5

6

7

8

ALWAYS DRAW EYES
AS OVALS AND THEN
REMOVE LIDS

Buford Van Stomm

Buford is the neighborhood bully who has grown into a buddy and become part of Phineas and Ferb's group of friends. He may not be the brightest guy around, but he knows more than you might think. He's a tough cookie (oatmeal raisin to be precise) and is rarely impressed.

1

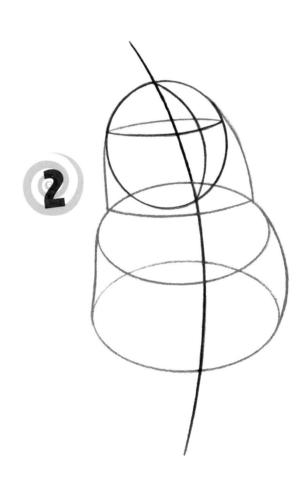

2

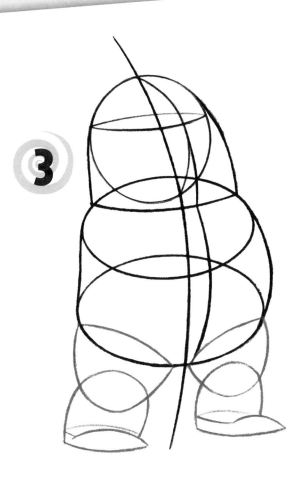

3

BUFORD HAS TWO NOTCHES IN HIS HAIR

KEEP HIS EYES ON ONE LINE

ONLY ONE TOOTH IS VISIBLE WHEN HIS MOUTH IS CLOSED — HOW DOES THIS GUY CHEW?

4

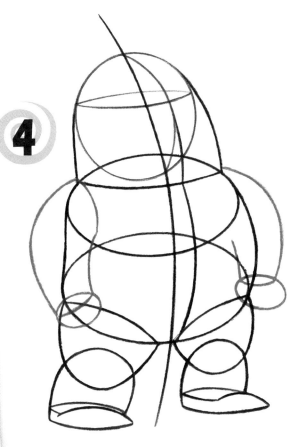

FRECKLES FORM A TRIANGLE

BUFORD HAS TEETH WHEN MOUTH IS OPEN

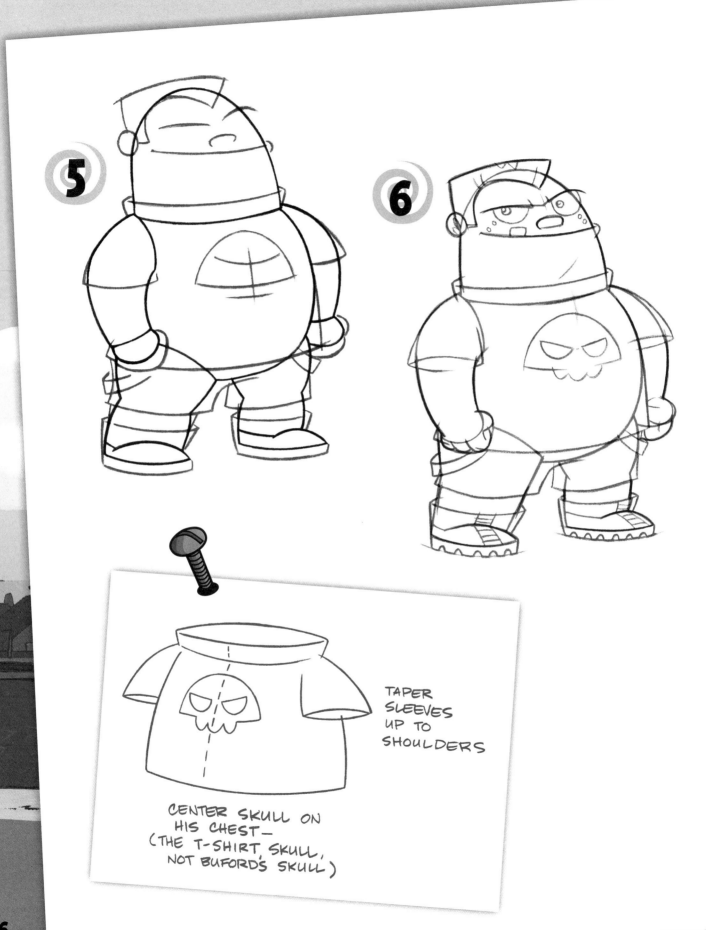

TAPER
SLEEVES
UP TO
SHOULDERS

CENTER SKULL ON
HIS CHEST—
(THE T-SHIRT SKULL,
NOT BUFORD'S SKULL)

Baljeet Rai

Baljeet is a mathematics and science whiz who values education above all else. (Hooray, school!) He is extremely intelligent, but more than a little sheltered. Once he's able to move past his insatiable need for schedules and grades, he can have as much fun as anyone.

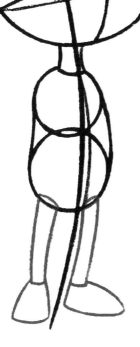

③

COLLAR IS A
HOOP SHAPE

KEEP A
SLIGHT "S"
CURVE TO
HIS BACK

CENTER
POCKET ON
HIS CENTERLINE

④

EYEBROWS ARE ON A CURVE

BACK OF HEAD HAS A SHARP EDGE LIKE HIS SLIDE RULE

USE "3" EAR DETAIL

KEEP HIS LEGS CURVED

NO SHOELACES

Jeremy Johnson

Jeremy is Candace's even-tempered crush. He can usually be found working at Slushee Dawg; teaching guitar lessons; or playing with his band, Jeremy and the Incidentals. He is very calm and unflappable…in direct contrast to Candace.

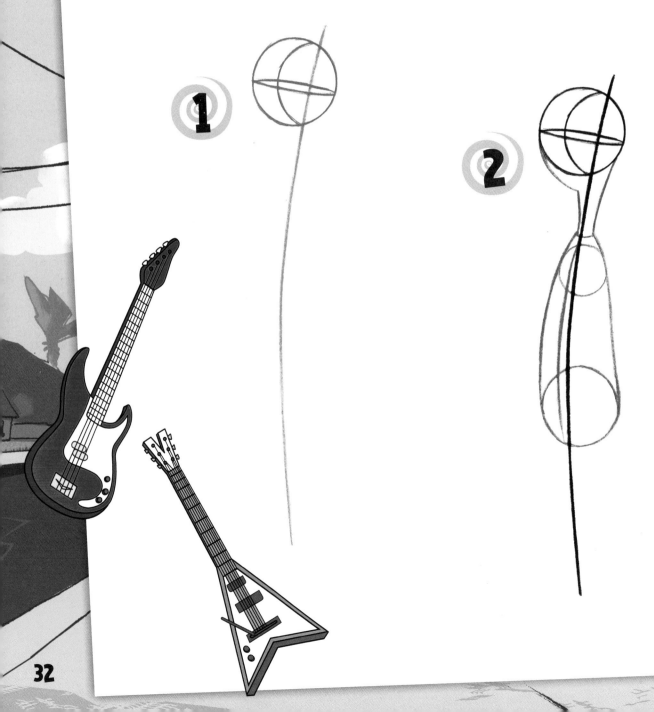

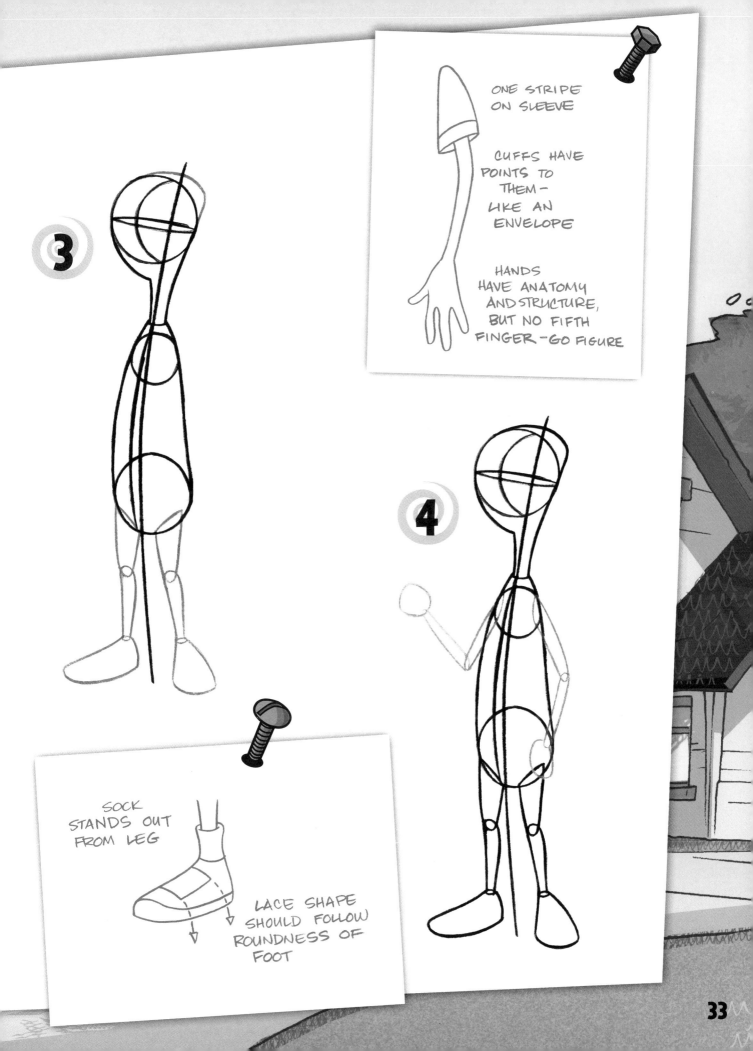

ONE STRIPE
ON SLEEVE

CUFFS HAVE
POINTS TO
THEM —
LIKE AN
ENVELOPE

HANDS
HAVE ANATOMY
AND STRUCTURE,
BUT NO FIFTH
FINGER — GO FIGURE

3

4

SOCK
STANDS OUT
FROM LEG

LACE SHAPE
SHOULD FOLLOW
ROUNDNESS OF
FOOT

Isabella Garcia-Shapiro

Isabella is the courageous, confident young lady who always greets her friends with a peppy, "Whatcha doin'?" As leader of the Fireside Girls, she is always prepared, resourceful, and ready to help—especially if it's Phineas who needs the help!

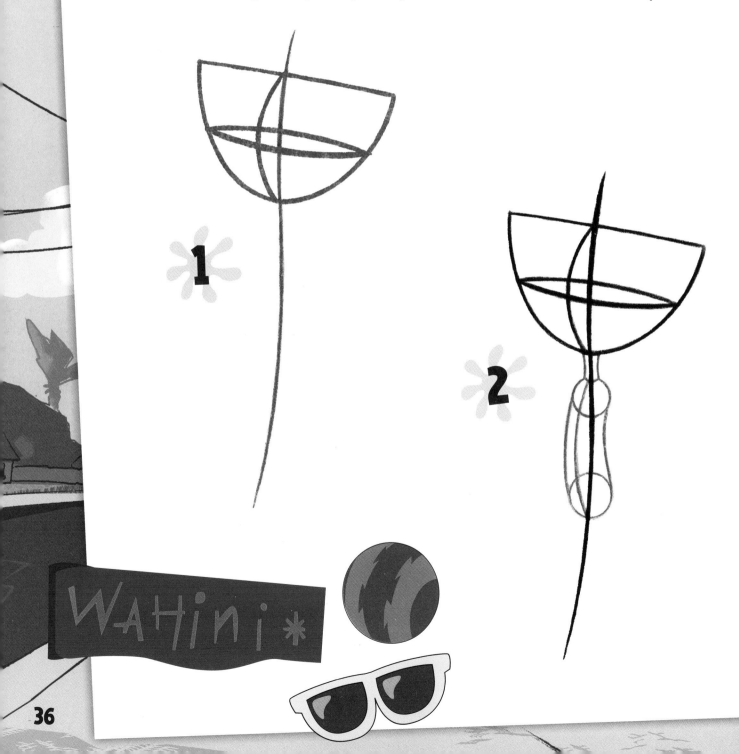

WAHINI *

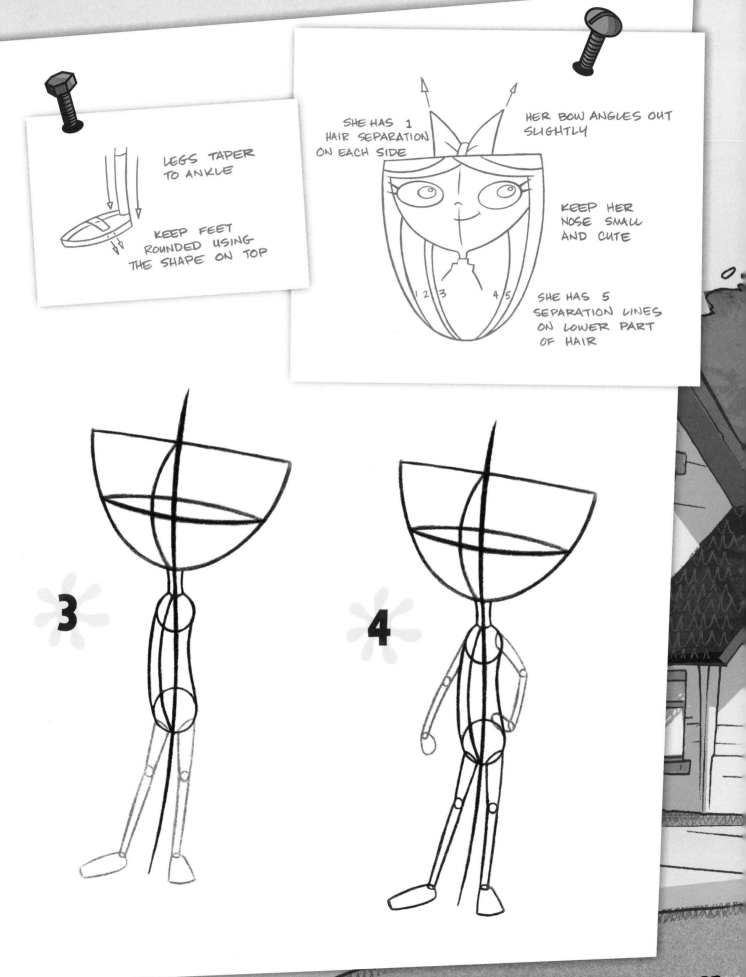

LEGS TAPER
TO ANKLE

KEEP FEET
ROUNDED USING
THE SHAPE ON TOP

SHE HAS 1
HAIR SEPARATION
ON EACH SIDE

HER BOW ANGLES OUT
SLIGHTLY

KEEP HER
NOSE SMALL
AND CUTE

1 2 3   4 5

SHE HAS 5
SEPARATION LINES
ON LOWER PART
OF HAIR

3

4

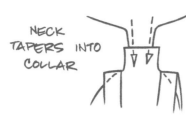

NECK
TAPERS INTO
COLLAR

SHOULDERS
ARE ROUND
UNDER DRESS

COLLAR AND DRESS ARE
SQUARED OFF

6

5

SHE HAS NO EYEBROWS (DON'T ASK.
SHE'S SENSITIVE ABOUT IT),
BUT HER BROW CAN BE USED
FOR EXPRESSIONS

7

BELT BUCKLE IS SLIGHTLY OVAL

1 2 3 4 5

HER SKIRT HAS 5 PLEATS

8

WAHINI *

Perry the Platypus

Perry is the Flynn-Fletcher family's beloved pet: a web-footed, egg-laying, semi-aquatic mammal who doesn't do much when the family is around. He likes to sit under a tree, sleep on the boys' beds, and occasionally make an odd platypus sound. Oh, and he's also known as a secret agent called Agent P.

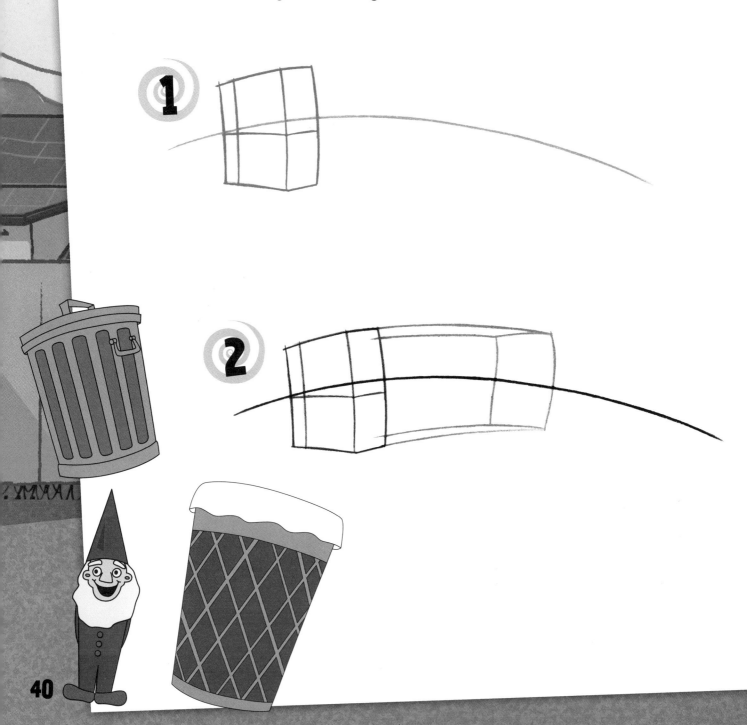

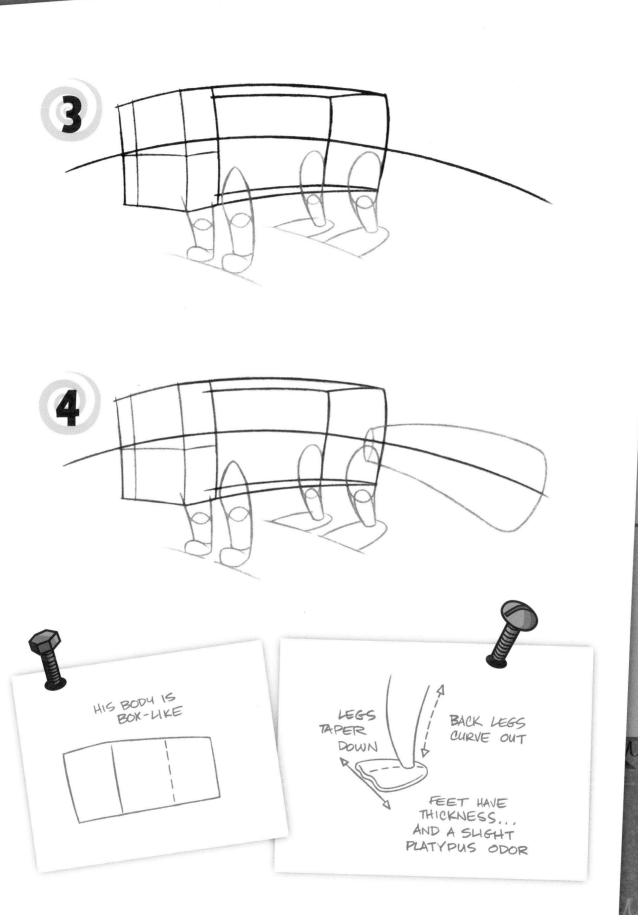

3

4

HIS BODY IS BOX-LIKE

LEGS TAPER DOWN

BACK LEGS CURVE OUT

FEET HAVE THICKNESS... AND A SLIGHT PLATYPUS ODOR

5

6

IT HELPS TO
LINE UP 3
DIAMONDS ON
THE CENTER LINE

1 2 3 4 5

1 2 3 4

THE TAIL
HAS THICKNESS—
IT IS NOT FLAT

HIS HIND END
IS FLAT AND HIS
TAIL CAN ROTATE,
WHICH IS BETTER
THAN THE
OTHER WAY
AROUND

3 HAIRS ARE CENTERED
ON HEAD WITH THE LONGEST
IN THE MIDDLE

EYES
SHOULD BE
A BIT OFF
KILTER

BILL HAS
MASS AND TAPERS
TO FACE

FRONT LEGS
CURVE IN

Agent P

Agent P is a secret agent of OWCA, operating from a hidden lair beneath Phineas and Ferb's house. He is brave, clever, and a master of platyjitsu, often using his tail as a lethal weapon against his nemesis, Dr. Doofenshmirtz.

3

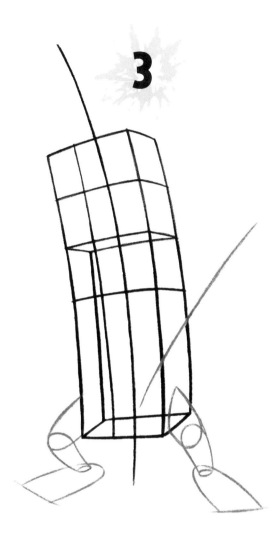

AGENT P
IS MADE UP
OF CURVES
(DESPITE
HAVING
NERVES OF
STEEL!)

4

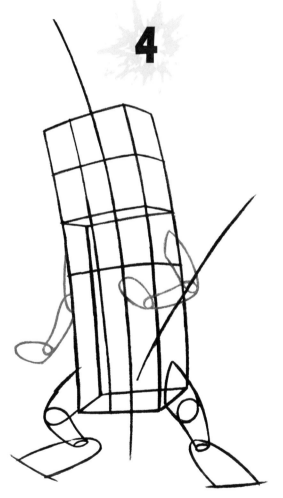

GIVE HIS FEET
THICKNESS AND
A BIT OF A CURVE WHEN
LIFTED OFF THE
GROUND

5

6

KEEP HIS HAT
WELL CONSTRUCTED

GIVE HIS HANDS
A LOT OF ENERGY
AND ATTITUDE

7

HE USUALLY HAS A DETERMINED EXPRESSION

HIS HAIR IS CENTERED ON HIS BOX-SHAPED HEAD

8

GIVE THE TAIL MASS, AND USE THE 3 DIAMOND METHOD TO FIGURE OUT THE SPACING

Linda Flynn–Fletcher

Linda is a busy mom who does more errands in one day than most people do in a month. She was once a pop star known as Lindana, but now she plays smooth jazz at the Squat N' Stitch. Her patience and dry sense of humor help her deal with Candace's constant interruptions.

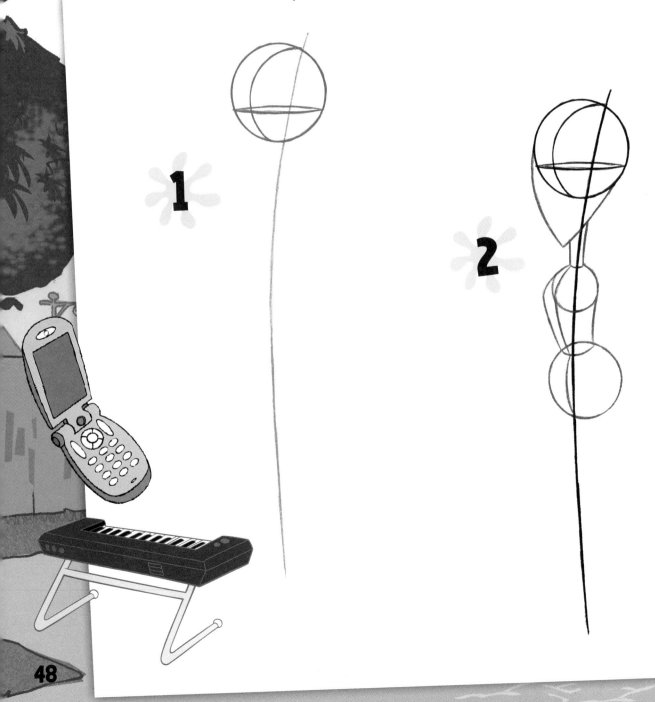

3

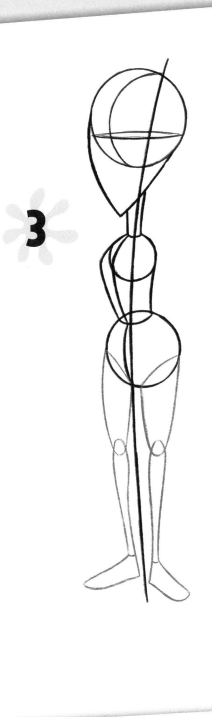

TAPER LEG
DOWN TO
ANKLE

CUFF IS
LARGER IN
FRONT

NO SOCKS!

4

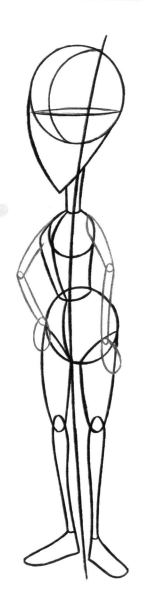

EYEBROW
GROWS FROM
CORNER OF
HER EYE

49

7

8

TOP OF NOSE
IS QUITE
STRAIGHT

SLIGHT CURVE UNDER NOSE—
REMEMBER, MOM NOSE BEST

Lawrence Fletcher

Lawrence, Phineas and Ferb's dad, hails from jolly old England. He runs an antique store in Danville, and he tells bad jokes. He is vaguely aware that his sons take on some major projects, which he thinks are "brilliant," in the most English sense of the word.

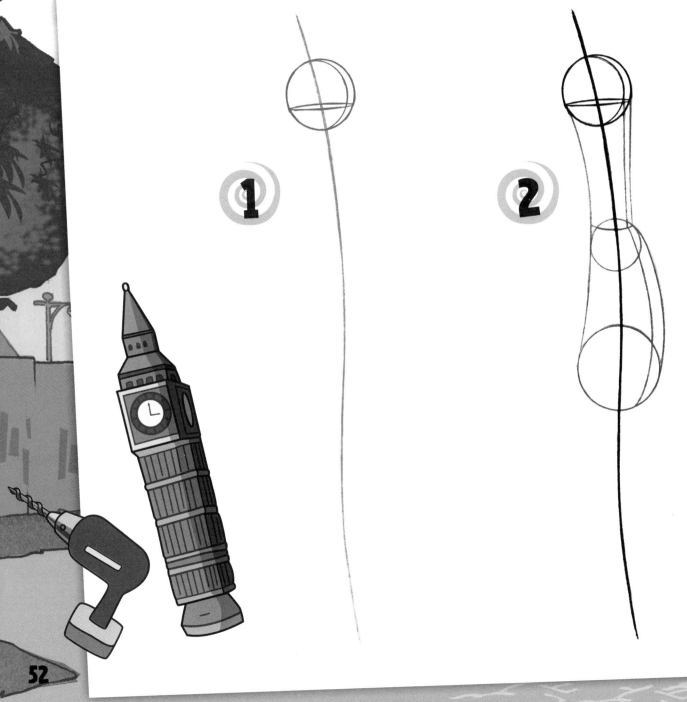

REMEMBER
HIS POCKET DETAIL
ON <u>HIS</u> LEFT

ONE STRIPE PER
SLEEVE

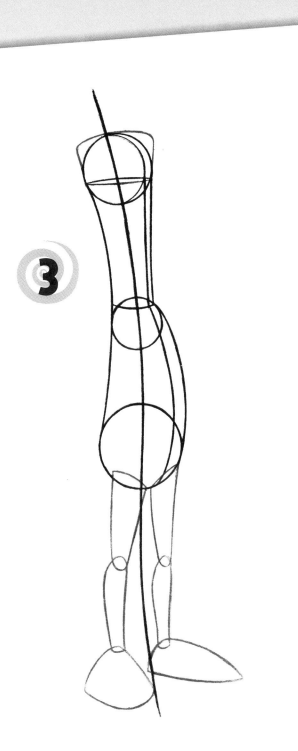

3

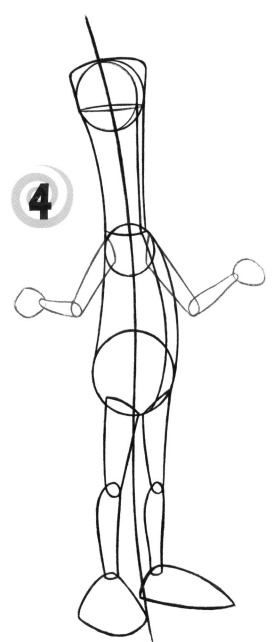

4

5

6

KEEP
HIS FEET
ROUND USING
SHOE DETAIL

DON'T LET
HIS NOSE GET
TOO SHARP

Dr. Heinz Doofenshmirtz

Doof is driven. He is tenacious. He is a talented inventor. If Agent P didn't show up to defeat him, he'd find a way to defeat himself. But despite constant failures, he will never give up on his dream to rule the entire Tri-State Area!

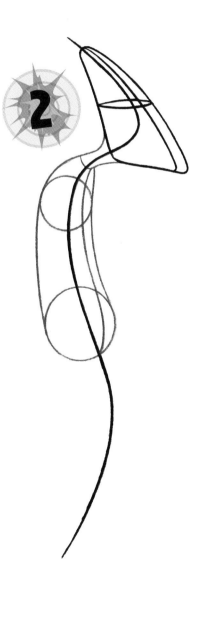

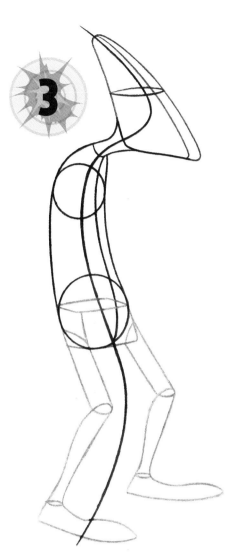

3

DOOF HAS
A HUNCHED
BACK

ARMS
ARE
ATTACHED
QUITE
LOW

4

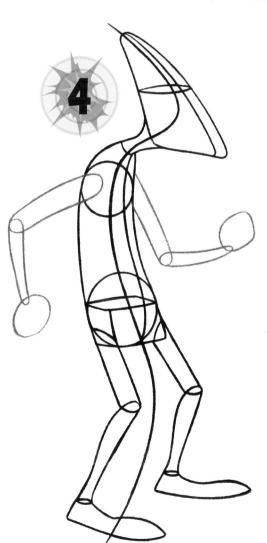

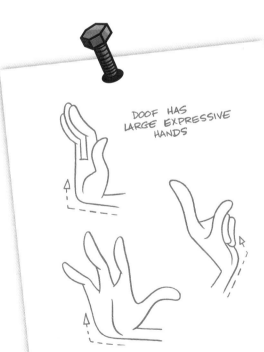

DOOF HAS
LARGE EXPRESSIVE
HANDS

DOOF HAS
6 LOCKS OF
HAIR

HE HAS
DARK CIRCLES
UNDER HIS
EYES

TEETH ARE
LARGE AND
OFF KILTER

COLLAR IS
A RING - NOT
FLAT

"3" IN EAR

5

6

HE OFTEN
STANDS WITH
KNEES BENT

Vanessa Doofenshmirtz

Vanessa is the cool daughter of Dr. Heinz Doofenshmirtz. She's a laid-back teen who dresses in all black and is rarely emotional except when her father mortifies her with his embarrassing antics. She knows he means well, but he's still a big doof.

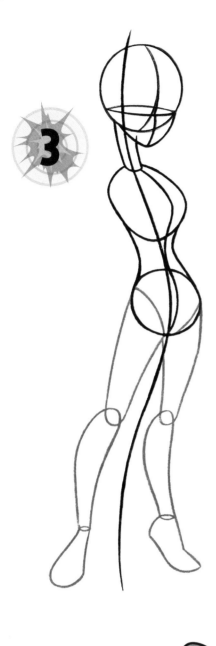

3

4

HER CUFFS ARE
POINTED AND WIDER
ON THE OUTSIDE

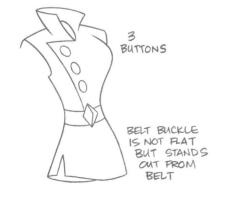

3
BUTTONS

BELT BUCKLE
IS NOT FLAT
BUT STANDS
OUT FROM
BELT

REMEMBER TO
USE THESE HAIR
LINES TO INDICATE
THE SHAPE OF
HER HEAD

KEEP EYELIDS
SOMEWHAT HEAVY

COLLAR IS
HIGH

SHOULDERS ARE
WIDE AND SQUARED
OFF

5

6

THESE BOOTS ARE
MADE FOR WALKING

BOOTS
FOLD OVER
AND COME TO
A POINT-
THEY ARE
LONGER IN
FRONT

HEELS ARE
HIGH

About the Illustrators

Greg Guler, a character designer for Disney's Emmy Award-winning animated series *Phineas and Ferb*, began drawing at a young age. Heralding from New Rockford, North Dakota, Greg studied commercial art in college and developed his natural abilities by spending many long hours at the drawing board. Greg's career path has taken him from graphic design to comic book illustration for such giants as DC Comics to the Walt Disney Studios in 1991 as a character designer for *Lilo & Stitch*, *Mickey Mouse Clubhouse*, and others. One of the original illustrators of *Phineas and Ferb*, Greg is honored to continue working with the show's talented cast and crew. He lives in Colorado with his beautiful wife, kids, and two beagles.

Nancy Ulene has been in the animation business for 30 years, the last 20 of which have been at the Disney Studios in Burbank, California. Nancy specializes in color styling, but she is also a sculptor and painter. She has been working on the show *Phineas and Ferb* since its inception and continues to work on every episode and movie. A single mom of two sons in college, Nancy has earned her stripes.

About the Writer

Scott Peterson is the author of many top-selling picture books in the *Phineas and Ferb* series, as well as the upcoming hardcover *Phineas and Ferb's Guide to Life*. For the last six years, Scott has worked as a story editor for Disney Television Animation on *Phineas and Ferb*, *Kick Buttowski*, *The Replacements*, and *Emperor's New School*. Scott was nominated for a 2006 primetime Emmy Award for Outstanding Animated Program for writing Nickelodeon's *Escape from Cluster Prime*. He lives in South Pasadena with his beautiful wife and two occasionally adorable children.